I Am Grateful For My Body

Written by Kristi Madeline Hyde
Illustrated by Nathalie Gelm

To my girls Wrynly, Arya, Lillian & Willow. I am grateful for you!

Copyright © 2020 by Kristi Madeline Hyde

All rights reserved. No part of this book may be reproduced or used in any manner without written permission of the copyright owners except for the use of quotations in a book review or for educational purposes.

To request permissions, contact the publisher at freedomhousepublishingco@gmail.com.

Hardcover: 978-1-952566-09-7
Paperback: 978-1-952566-07-3
Ebook: 978-1-952566-08-0

Words by Kristi Madeline Hyde
Illustrations by Nathalie Gelm

Printed in the USA.

I have learned that being grateful for what we have, even if it is the smallest things, helps us to feel lighter, shine brighter, and have a more positive outlook on life. Naming the thing we are grateful for, closing our eyes and feeling our gratitude and why we are grateful, then saying thank you three times really puts us into a positive perspective.

As you read this book with your children, ask them what they are grateful for and why. You will be surprised at the beauty of gratitude that lies within them and you!

I am grateful for **my eyes** because I can see the shapes in the clouds.

I am grateful for **my mouth** because I can speak kindly to myself.

Thank you!

Thank you!

Thank you!

I am grateful for **my ears** because I can hear my brother singing.

Thank you!

Thank you!

Thank you!

Thank you!

Thank you!

Thank you!

I am grateful for **my heart**

because it helps me to love.

Thank you!

Thank you!

Thank you!

I am grateful for **my hands**

because I can draw my favorite things.

Thank you!

Thank you!

Thank you!

I am grateful for **my body** because my body is amazing!

About the Author

Kristi Madeline Hyde lives in Utah with the love of her life and four amazing, crazy girls. She is most grateful for her family, crystals, cats, and her hands - because they make magical things. You can connect with her on Instagram @KristiMadelineHyde or visit www.Kristimadelinehyde.com

About the Illustrator

Nathalie Gelm has always loved art and illustrating. She graduated from the Academy of Arts and fell in love with drawing pictures for children. She is grateful for her fingers because she can hold pencils and draw pictures. You can connect with her on Instagram @Coovieboo

ACKNOWLEDGMENTS

I am grateful for my husband, Jarom, who has been my rock and super supporter throughout everything. These past 14 years have been a dream.

I am grateful for my girls who push boundaries, teach me patience, and show me that gratitude is fun, simple, can help relieve bad dreams and angry attitudes, and fill our hearts with love.

I am forever grateful to Keira Poulsen who helped me to find the thing that brings me joy and healing, and showed me how to step into my Divinity.

I am grateful for The Magic by Rhonda Byrne for teaching me how to feel gratitude and be grateful every day, not just when good things happen. I'm hoping to bring her magic to children everywhere! Thank you! Thank you! Thank you!

www.ingramcontent.com/pod-product-compliance
Lightning Source LLC
Chambersburg PA
CBHW041459220426

43661CB00016B/1195